Healthcare Job Pack

D0224596

Living and Working in English

Joan Saslow

Tim Collins

Job Pack by
Kristin Sherman

Longman

Workplace Plus: Living and Working in English 1 and 2
Healthcare Job Pack

Pearson Education, 10 Bank Street, White Plains, NY 10606

Vice president, instructional design: Allen Ascher
Senior acquisitions editor: Marian Wassner
Senior development editor: Marcia Schonzeit
Development editor: Peter Benson
Vice president, director of design and production: Rhea Banker
Executive managing editor: Linda Moser
Production manager: Liza Pleva
Senior production editor: Christine Lauricella
Associate production editor: Scott Fava
Director of manufacturing: Patrice Fraccio
Senior manufacturing buyer: Dave Dickey
Cover design: Ann France
Text design and composition: Rainbow Graphics
Text art: Rainbow Graphics, Wendy Wolf

ISBN: 0-13-098318-7

Printed in the United States of America
1 2 3 4 5 6 7 8 9 10—PBT—07 06 05 04 03 02

Contents

To the teacher

This *Workplace Plus Healthcare Job Pack* can be used in conjunction with *Workplace Plus 1* and *2* to expand the general language introduced in the series to the specific needs of healthcare professionals. This supplement will help learners comprehend spoken and written English related to healthcare, and will afford learners practice in communicating in a healthcare setting. It will also help learners understand the expectations of the healthcare workplace.

Contents

The *Job Pack* consists of 20 units: ten units that correspond to *Workplace Plus 1*, followed by ten units that correspond to *Workplace Plus 2*. Each *Job Pack* unit is related to the theme of the corresponding unit in *Workplace Plus* and builds on the language and skills developed in that unit, allowing learners to extend their competencies to the specific career field of healthcare. For example, in Unit 7 of *Workplace Plus 1*, learners communicate about current tasks and obligations. In Unit 7 of the *Healthcare Job Pack Level 1*, learners communicate about specific tasks and obligations related to caring for patients, perhaps as a nursing assistant or a residential aide. The *Job Pack* also includes a list of common abbreviations and a metric conversion chart.

Format

Each unit is a two-page sheet, with the *Word bank* and *Conversations* appearing on the first page, and *Authentic practice* on the second.

1. *Word bank*
   Essential vocabulary for the unit is presented.

2. *Conversations*
   Model conversations similar to those in *Workplace Plus* are adapted to the healthcare setting.

3. *Authentic practice*
   Real-world examples allow learners to practice communication skills in a healthcare context. All examples involve reading and understanding authentic texts from the workplace and performing purposeful tasks based on them. In some units, learners create and rehearse conversations; in other units, they practice writing.

How to use the Job Pack

The *Healthcare Job Pack* allows the teacher to tailor instruction to the needs of a particular class.

- **Single occupation focus:** In some classes, all the learners may be training for the healthcare field. Teachers can move freely between the *Workplace Plus* books and this *Job Pack,* perhaps having learners practice the pair work conversations immediately after the model conversations in the text, thereby reinforcing the basic language structures while introducing job-specific vocabulary.

- **Multiple occupation focus:** In some settings, the learners in a single class may be preparing for different occupations. The *Workplace Plus* series enables the instructor to teach essential language and life skills to all the learners together, while the *Healthcare Job Pack* can be assigned to those learners who are training for the healthcare field. Other *Job Packs* can be used by learners training for other occupations.

- **Self-access learning environment:** The *Job Pack* can also be used in a self-access learning environment such as a language lab. Learners can be partnered in the lab, and then complete units independently, outside the *Workplace Plus* classroom.

WORKPLACE PLUS 1

Unit 1

➤ Word bank

Occupations

a nurse	a receptionist
a doctor	a supervisor
a nurse's aide / a nursing assistant	a technician
a service aide	a pharmacist
an escort	a home health aide
a kitchen aide	

Other words

new	a shift
male	a staffing schedule
female	an employee
a position	

DO IT YOURSELF!   **Add your <u>own</u> words to the lists.**

_____   _____   _____

_____   _____   _____

➤ Conversations

❶ Talk about names and occupations.

A. **Read the conversation with a partner.**

A: Are you Kathy Lopez?
B: No, I'm not. I'm Mary Baker.
A: What do you do?
B: I'm a pharmacist.
A: Oh, hi! Good to meet you. I'm Martin Fletcher. I'm a technician.
B: Nice to meet you, Martin.

B. **PAIR WORK.**   **Now use the word bank or your <u>own</u> words.**

A: Are you Kathy Lopez?
B: No, I'm not. I'm _____.
A: What do you do?
B: I'm _____.
A: Oh, hi! Good to meet you. I'm _____. I'm _____.
B: Nice to meet you, _____.

❷ Greet an employee.

A. **Read the conversation with a partner.**

A: May I help you, please?
B: Yes, I'm Sharon Wells.
A: Nice to meet you, Sharon. Are you the new kitchen aide?
B: Yes, I am.
A: Welcome. Please fill out this form.

B. **PAIR WORK.**   **Now use the word bank or your <u>own</u> words.**

A: May I help you, please?
B: Yes, I'm _____.
A: Nice to meet you, _____. Are you the new _____?
B: Yes, I am.
A: Welcome. Please fill out this form.

A. Look at the staffing schedules.

Staffing schedule 7 a.m.–3 p.m. shift

Male employees	Position
Mwangi, Rene	Nurse
Signa, Pat	Service aide
Williams, Jim	Nursing assistant
Woods, Andy	Escort

Staffing schedule 7 a.m.–3 p.m. shift

Female employees	Position
Aremu, Kiki	Nurse
Martin, Cathy	Nursing assistant
Robertson, Ann	Nursing assistant
Thomas, Lisa	Service aide

Write <u>yes</u> or <u>no</u> after each sentence.

1. Jim Williams is a nurse. _____

2. Ann Robertson is a nursing assistant. _____

3. Pat Signa is an escort. _____

4. Rene Mwangi is a service aide. _____

B. Now answer questions about the employees.

1. Is Kiki Aremu a nurse or a nursing assistant? _____

2. What is Cathy Martin's occupation? _____

3. What does Andy Woods do? _____

C. ROLE PLAY. **With a partner, create a conversation. Ask and answer questions about the employees in the staffing schedules.**

Unit 2

➤ Word bank

Rooms and workplaces

a nursing station	a lounge	an elevator	a unit
a dining room / a cafeteria	a waiting room	a radiology department	a hospital
a gift shop	a kitchen	an emergency room	a clinic
a recreation room	a shower room	an outpatient department	a nursing home
a chapel	a lobby	a pharmacy	a floor plan

DO IT YOURSELF!   **Add your <u>own</u> words to the list.**

_____   _____   _____

_____   _____   _____

➤ Conversations

❶ **Talk about places.**

A. Read the conversation with a partner.

A: Is Ann here?
B: No, she's not. She's in the lounge.
A: Where's the lounge?
B: It's next to the elevator.
A: Thanks.

B. PAIR WORK.   Now use the word bank or your <u>own</u> words.

A: Is _____ here?
B: No, _____ not. _____.
A: Where's the _____?
B: _____.
A: _____.

❷ **Give directions.**

A. Read the conversation with a partner.

A: Excuse me. Where is the chapel?
B: It's down the hall, across from the nursing station.
A: Across from the nursing station?
B: Yes.
A: Thank you.
B: No problem.

B. PAIR WORK.   Now use the word bank or your <u>own</u> words.

A: Excuse me. Where is the _____?
B: It's down the hall, _____.
A: _____?
B: Yes.
A: _____.
B: _____.

A. Look at the hospital floor plan.

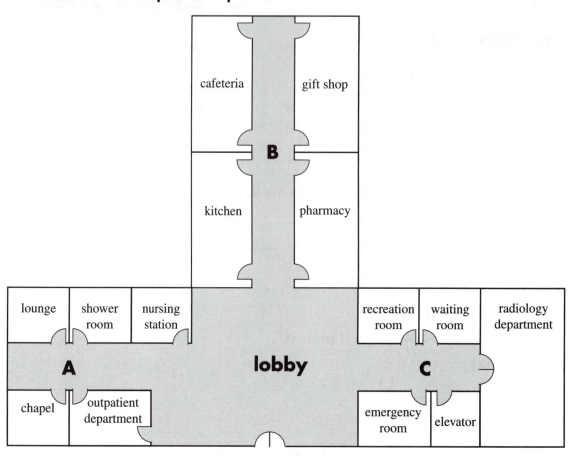

Write the letter of the hall where each place is located.

1. the radiology department   _____
2. the shower room   _____
3. the cafeteria   _____
4. the pharmacy   _____
5. the recreation room   _____

B. Give directions. Use words from the box and your <u>own</u> words. Then practice your conversation with a partner.

next to	across from	between	on A hall

1. A: Where's the emergency room?

   B: _____

2. A: Where's the outpatient department?

   B: _____

3. A: Where's the elevator?

   B: _____

C. Role Play.   With a partner, create a new conversation. Ask for and give directions. Use the hospital floor plan in Exercise A.

Unit 3

➤ Word bank

Fixtures and furnishings

a toilet	a bed
a shower	an overbed table
a sink	a bedside stand
a handle	a chair
a lever	a call system
a television	privacy curtains
a stretcher	bedrails
an IV pole	

Actions

move
raise
lower
use
get

Directions

to the right
to the left

DO IT YOURSELF!   **Add your <u>own</u> words to the lists.**

_____   _____   _____

_____   _____   _____

➤ Conversations

❶ Make a suggestion. Get help.

A. With a partner, read the conversation between two healthcare workers.

A: Oh, no!
B: What's wrong?
A: The shower is out of order.
B: Let's call the nurse.
A: Good idea.

B. PAIR WORK.   Now use the word bank or your <u>own</u> words.

A: Oh, no!
B: What's wrong?
A: The _____ is out of order.
B: Let's call _____.
A: Good idea.

❷ Give directions. Give a warning.

A. Read the conversations with a partner.

A: Please raise the bed.
B: OK.

A: Don't lower the bedrails.
B: No problem.

B. PAIR WORK.   Now use the word bank or your <u>own</u> words.

A: Please _____ the _____.
B: _____.

A: Don't _____ the _____.
B: _____.

A. **Look at the directions on a hospital telephone and a hospital bed.**

Housekeeping	Press 6 + 5542
Food Service	Press 6 + 5322
Medical Equipment	Press 6 + 3327
Supply	Press 6 + 9225
Outside calls	Press 9 + area code + phone #

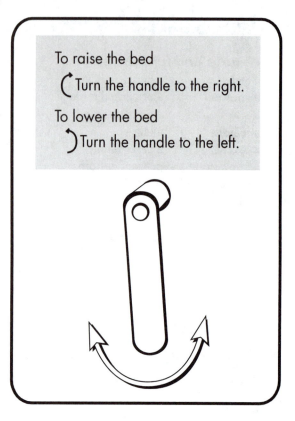

To raise the bed
Turn the handle to the right.

To lower the bed
Turn the handle to the left.

Write yes or no after each sentence.

1. To call Housekeeping, press 6 + 5542. _____

2. To call Food Service, press 6 + 5322. _____

3. To call Supply, press 6 + 3327. _____

4. To raise the bed, turn the handle to the left. _____

B. **Give directions to a co-worker. Then practice your conversation with a partner.**

1. A: How do I call Medical Equipment?

   B: _____

2. A: How do I make an outside call?

   B: _____

3. A: How do I lower the bed?

   B: _____

C. ROLE PLAY.   **With a partner, create a new conversation. Ask for and give directions. Use the directions on the telephone and on the bed.**

Unit 4

➤ Word bank

Clothes		Colors	Other adjectives	Actions
a nightgown	pajamas	pink	clean / dirty	wash
a bra	socks	purple	pressed / wrinkled	press
a robe	slippers	gray		
a sweater	underpants			
an undershirt				

DO IT YOURSELF!   **Add your own words to the lists.**

_____   _____   _____

_____   _____   _____

➤ Conversations

❶ Offer help. Ask about size and color.

A. With a partner, read the conversation between a healthcare worker and a patient.

A: Hi, Mrs. Jordan. May I help you?
B: Yes, please. I need a robe.
A: What size?
B: Small. And I need pajamas.
A: What color?
B: Yellow, please.

B. PAIR WORK.   Now use the word bank or your own words.

A: Hi, _____. May I help you?
B: Yes, please. I need _____.
A: What size?
B: _____. And I need _____.
A: What color?
B: _____.

❷ Talk about problems with clothes.

A. With a partner, read the conversation between a patient and a healthcare worker.

A: Excuse me. This sweater is dirty.
B: Oh, I'm sorry. Here is a clean sweater.
A: Thanks.

B. PAIR WORK.   Now use the word bank or your own words.

A: Excuse me. _____.
B: Oh, I'm sorry. Here _____.
A: Thanks.

A. **Look at the patient's laundry list. Then answer the questions.**

Name: Mrs. Fran Jordan			Room: 425
Item	**Color**	**Please wash**	**Please press**
sweater	purple	☒	☐
pants	gray	☐	☒
nightgown	pink	☒	☐
socks	white	☒	☐
robe	red	☐	☒

1. What color is the sweater? _____

2. What color are the pants? _____

3. What color is the nightgown? _____

4. What's the problem with the robe? _____

B. **Respond to each problem.**

1. This nightgown is dirty.

   _____

2. These slippers are too small.

   _____

3. This robe is wrinkled.

   _____

C. **Use the information to fill out a laundry list for Mr. Franklin in Room 457.**

The white undershirt is dirty. The purple shirt is dirty and wrinkled. The gray pajamas are dirty.

Name:			Room:
Item	**Color**	**Please wash**	**Please press**
undershirt		☐	☐
shirt		☐	☐
pajamas		☐	☐

Unit 5

➤ Word bank

Activities

board games	bridge	indoor gardening
music	photography	painting
baking	drawing	drama
yoga	pet care	stretching

DO IT YOURSELF! **Add your own words to the list.**

_____ _____ _____

_____ _____ _____

➤ Conversations

❶ Talk about times and activities.

A. Read the conversation with a partner.

A: What time is it?
B: It's 2:30.
A: 2:30? Uh-oh. I'm late for yoga. Bye.
B: Bye. See you later.

B. PAIR WORK.   Now use the word bank or your own words.

A: What time is it?
B: It's _____.
A: _____? Uh-oh. I'm late for _____. Bye.
B: Bye. See you later.

❷ Talk about schedules.

A. With a partner, read the conversation between a patient and a healthcare worker.

A: What time does pet care start?
B: At 11 a.m.
A: And when does it end?
B: I'm not sure. At noon, I think.
A: At noon? That's great!

B. PAIR WORK.   Now use the word bank or your own words.

A: What time does _____ start?
B: At _____.
A: And when does it end?
B: I'm not sure. At _____, I think.
A: At _____? That's great!

A. Read the schedule of activities at a nursing home. Then write the letter of the place next to each activity.

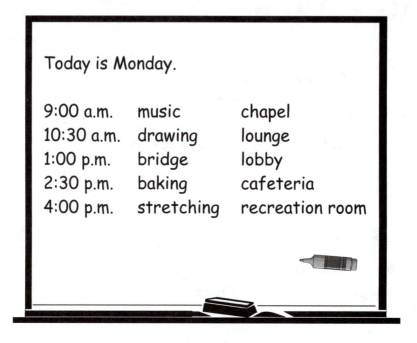

Today is Monday.

9:00 a.m.   music   chapel
10:30 a.m.   drawing   lounge
1:00 p.m.   bridge   lobby
2:30 p.m.   baking   cafeteria
4:00 p.m.   stretching   recreation room

1. _____ music   a. in the recreation room

2. _____ stretching   b. in the lounge

3. _____ bridge   c. in the chapel

4. _____ drawing   d. in the cafeteria

5. _____ baking   e. in the lobby

B. Answer a patient's questions about activities. Then practice the conversation with a partner.

1. A: When do we have baking?

   B: _____

2. A: Where do we have stretching today?

   B: _____

3. A: What activity is at 10:30?

   B: _____

C. ROLE PLAY.   With a partner, create a new conversation. Ask and answer questions about the schedule of activities.

Unit 6

➤ Word bank

Foods

Jell-O	salad	a banana
cereal	peas	a vegetable
soup	pork	a roll
applesauce	butter	
ice cream		

Meals and other words

breakfast	dessert
lunch	a snack
dinner	a menu

DO IT YOURSELF!   **Add your <u>own</u> words to the lists.**

_____   _____   _____

_____   _____   _____

➤ Conversations

❶ Talk about a meal.

A. **With a partner, read the conversation between a patient and a healthcare worker.**

A: Hi, Maria. Do you have my breakfast?
B: Yes. What do you want first?
A: Cereal, please.
B: Do you want a banana, too?
A: Yes, I love bananas.

B. **PAIR WORK.**   **Now use the word bank or your <u>own</u> words.**

A: Hi, _____. Do you have my _____?
B: Yes. What do you want first?
A: _____, please.
B: Do you want _____, too?
A: _____.

❷ Talk about a menu.

A. **With a partner, read the conversation between a healthcare worker and a patient.**

A: Hi, Mrs. Johnson. What do you want for dinner tomorrow?
B: Do you have a menu?
A: Sure. Here it is.
B: I want pork.
A: OK. Anything else?
B: Yes. Salad and peas, please.

B. **PAIR WORK.**   **Now use the word bank or your <u>own</u> words.**

A: Hi, _____. What do you want for _____?
B: Do you have a menu?
A: Sure. Here it is.
B: I want _____.
A: _____. Anything else?
B: Yes. _____ and _____, please.

A. Read the patient's lunch menu. Then write <u>true</u> or <u>false</u> after each sentence.

> Please check what patient wants below.
> Name: <u>Kathryn Marks</u>   Type of diet: <u>Regular</u>
>
> Bread ☐   Rolls ☒   Butter ☒
>
> | **Soup** | Vegetable ☒ | Chicken ☐ |
> |---|---|---|
> | **Meat** | Chicken ☐ | Pork ☒ |
> | **Vegetables** | Carrots ☐ | Peas ☒ |
> | **Dessert** | Ice cream ☒ | Jell-O ☐ |
> | **Drinks** | Milk ☒ | Juice ☐ |

1. The patient wants vegetable soup.   _____

2. Kathryn Marks wants chicken for lunch.   _____

3. Then she wants Jell-O for dessert.   _____

4. Kathryn Marks wants milk for her drink.   _____

B. Answer a patient's questions about the menu.

1. Is there any applesauce on the menu?

   _____

2. Are there any rolls for lunch?

   _____

3. What vegetables are on the menu?

   _____

C. ROLE PLAY.   With a partner, create a conversation between a healthcare worker and a patient. Talk about the menu. Help the patient fill out the menu.

> Please check what patient wants below.
> Name: _____   Type of diet: _____
>
> Bread ☐   Rolls ☐   Butter ☐
>
> | **Soup** | Vegetable ☐ | Chicken ☐ |
> |---|---|---|
> | **Meat** | Chicken ☐ | Pork ☐ |
> | **Vegetables** | Carrots ☐ | Peas ☐ |
> | **Dessert** | Ice cream ☐ | Jell-O ☐ |
> | **Drinks** | Milk ☐ | Juice ☐ |

Unit 7

➤ Word bank

Actions with patients
bathe
feed
dress
transport
check on

Other actions at work
empty trash
pass ice
supervise the meal
assist with feeding

DO IT YOURSELF!   **Add your own words to the lists.**

_____   _____   _____

_____   _____   _____

➤ Conversations

❶ Talk about what you have to do.

A. **With a partner, read the conversation between a supervisor and a nursing assistant.**

A: Can you bathe Mrs. Martin?
B: No, I'm sorry, I can't.
A: Why not?
B: Because I have to feed Mr. Chen.
A: Well, when can you bathe Mrs. Martin?
B: In 20 minutes.

B. **PAIR WORK.**   **Now use the word bank or your own words.**

A: Can you _____?
B: No, I'm sorry, I can't.
A: Why not?
B: Because I have to _____.
A: Well, when can you _____?
B: In _____.

❷ Talk about what you're doing.

A. **Read the conversation with a partner.**

A: Are you busy right now?
B: Yes, I am.
A: What are you doing?
B: I'm emptying the trash.

B. **PAIR WORK.**   **Now use the word bank or your own words.**

A: Are you busy right now?
B: Yes, I am.
A: What are you doing?
B: I'm _____.

A. Read the duty chart. Then write the name of the nursing assistant next to each duty.

Nursing Assistants	Unit Duties
Gooden, Marsha	Clean dining room after meal. Pass ice on C hall.
Kidane, Hailemichael	Clean kitchen. Empty trash.
Leonard, Brenda	Clean lounge. Supervise dining room meal.
Martin, Ricky	Clean shower room. Pass ice on A hall.
Reyes, Gloria	Assist with feeding in dining room.

1. Pass ice on A hall. _____

2. Empty trash. _____

3. Supervise dining room meal. _____

4. Clean dining room after meal. _____

B. Answer the questions about the nursing assistants' duties. Then practice the conversations with a partner.

1. A: Hi, I'm Brenda. What do I have to do today?

   B: _____

2. A: Hi, I'm Ricky. What are my unit duties?

   B: _____

3. A: Hi, Gloria. What are your unit duties?

   B: _____

C. ROLE PLAY. With a partner, create a conversation. Ask and answer questions about unit duties. Use the duty chart in Exercise A.

Unit 8

➤ Word bank

Falls
in the bathroom
from a wheelchair
while walking
while standing

Injuries
a fracture
a sprain
a cut
a bruise

DO IT YOURSELF!   **Add your <u>own</u> words to the lists.**

_____   _____   _____

_____   _____   _____

➤ Conversations

❶ Report an accident.

A. **Read the conversation with a partner.**

A: Nursing station.
B: This is Elizabeth in room 312. Mr. Murphy had a fall from the bed.
A: Do you need a nurse or a nurse's aide?
B: A nurse, please.
A: OK. A nurse is on the way.

B. PAIR WORK.   **Now use the word bank or your <u>own</u> words.**

A: Nursing station.
B: This is _____ in room _____. _____ had a fall _____.
A: Do you need _____ or _____?
B: _____, please.
A: OK. _____ is on the way.

❷ Talk about an injury.

A. **Read the conversation with a partner.**

A: This is the nursing station. How can I help you?
B: I had a fall.
A: Oh, I'm sorry. What's wrong?
B: I hurt my back. I think I have a sprain.
A: Someone is on the way.

B. PAIR WORK.   **Now use the word bank or your <u>own</u> words.**

A: This is the nursing station. How can I help you?
B: I had a fall.
A: Oh, I'm sorry. What's wrong?
B: I hurt my _____. I think I have a _____.
A: _____ is on the way.

A. Read the accident report. Then check <u>yes</u> or <u>no</u> after each sentence.

**TO REPORT A SERIOUS ACCIDENT IMMEDIATELY OR FOR QUESTIONS,
PLEASE CALL RISK MANAGEMENT AT 555-3222**

1. Name of person injured: <u>Ms. Barbara Harris</u>   2. Sex: ☐ male ☑ female

ACCIDENT

3. Date: <u>9/10/03</u>   4. Time: <u>3:15 p.m.</u>   5. Location: <u>Room 636</u>

6. FALLS

☑ while walking   ☐ while standing   ☐ from chair / wheelchair
☐ from bed / stretcher   ☐ in bathroom

7. INJURY (check all that apply)

☐ fracture   ☑ sprain   ☐ cut   ☐ bruise

---

	yes	no
1. The accident was at 9:10 a.m.	☐	☐
2. The accident was in the lounge.	☐	☐
3. The patient had a fall while walking.	☐	☐
4. The injury was a sprain.	☐	☐

**B. Use the following information to fill out the accident report. Compare reports
with a partner.**

On May 15, 2003, Mr. James Braxton fell in the bathroom of room 411. It was 2:30 in the
afternoon. He had an ankle fracture and some bruises.

**TO REPORT A SERIOUS ACCIDENT IMMEDIATELY OR FOR QUESTIONS,
PLEASE CALL RISK MANAGEMENT AT 555-3222**

1. Name of person injured: _____   2. Sex: ☐ male ☐ female

ACCIDENT

3. Date: _____   4. Time: _____   5. Location: _____

6. FALLS

☐ while walking   ☐ while standing   ☐ from chair / wheelchair
☐ from bed / stretcher   ☐ in bathroom

7. INJURY (check all that apply)

☐ fracture   ☐ sprain   ☐ cut   ☐ bruise

Unit 9

➤ Word bank

Items used by healthcare workers

a name plate   a mask
a hairnet   support hose
a watch   rubber gloves
a lab coat   orthopedic shoes
a stethoscope

DO IT YOURSELF!   **Add your <u>own</u> words to the lists.**

_____   _____   _____

_____   _____   _____

➤ Conversations

❶ Ask for a price.

A. Read the conversation with a partner.

A: Excuse me. How much is this lab coat?
B: $22.99.
A: That's too expensive. I'll have to think about it.

B. PAIR WORK.   Now use the word bank or your <u>own</u> words.

A: Excuse me. How much is this _____?
B: _____.
A: That's _____. I'll have to think about it.

❷ Agree to buy something.

A. Read the conversation with a partner.

A: How much are these pants?
B: Only $12.59. They're on sale.
A: Great. I'll take them.
B: Will that be cash or charge?
A: Cash.

B. PAIR WORK.   Now use the word bank or your <u>own</u> words.

A: How much are these _____?
B: Only _____. They're on sale.
A: Great. I'll take them.
B: Will that be cash or charge?
A: _____.

A. Read the credit card bill. Then answer the questions.

Statement of Vista Card Account *VISTA*

Account Number	Statement Closing Date	Total Amount Due
1001-986253-58731	08/25/03	$24.99

Dr. Denise Kitterman
1322 North Lake Dr.
Collier, ND 33992

Previous balance $.00	New charges $24.99	Other debits $.00	Balance due $24.99

Item number	Description of monthly activity	Charges	Credits
1	Tiptoe Shoes 8/20/03	$24.99	$.00

1. Who is the customer? _____

2. On what date did she use the credit card? _____

3. What did the customer buy? _____

4. How much is the bill for? _____

B. Read the credit card bill. Then write a check to pay the bill. Use today's date and your <u>own</u> signature.

Statement of Vista Card Account *VISTA*

Account Number	Statement Closing Date	Total Amount Due
8360-669097-77010	10/25/03	$16.55

Previous balance $.00	New charges $16.55	Other debits $.00	Balance due $16.55

Item number	Description of monthly activity	Charges	Credits
1	Time Flies watch 10/14/03	$16.55	$.00

No. 487

DATE _____

PAY TO THE
ORDER OF _____ $ [ ]

_____ DOLLARS

United Bank
1550 Fourth Ave.
Sacramento, CA 95819

MEMO _____   _____

1:041000689:1   60660668'   487

Unit 10

➤ Word bank

Occupations	Skills
1. a service aide	makes beds / passes out meal trays
2. a kitchen aide	helps prepare food / helps the cook
3. a dietary aide	checks menus / prepares food trays
4. an escort	pushes wheelchairs / helps patients walk
5. a laboratory technician (lab tech)	works with equipment / does tests
6. a registered nurse (RN)	cares for sick people / passes out medicine
7. a pharmacist	works in a pharmacy / prepares medicine
8. a home health aide	prepares meals / helps patients with personal care
9. a physical therapist	helps patients with injuries / gives patients exercises
10. certified nursing assistant (CNA)	helps feed patients / helps with personal care

DO IT YOURSELF!   **Add your _own_ words to the lists.**

_____   _____   _____

_____   _____   _____

➤ Conversations

❶ Talk about skills.

A. Read the conversation with a partner.

A: I'm looking for a job in a hospital.
B: OK. Do you have any experience?
A: Yes. I was a dietary aide for two years.
B: Can you prepare food trays?
A: Of course. I can check menus too.
B: Great! Do you want to fill out an application?

B. PAIR WORK.   Now use the word bank or your _own_ words.

A: I'm looking for a job _____.
B: OK. Do you have any experience?
A: Yes. I was _____ for _____.
B: Can you _____?
A: Of course. I can _____ too.
B: _____! Do you want to fill out an application?

❷ Talk about past experience.

A. Read the conversation with a partner.

A: So, Ms. Gomaa, what did you do in Egypt?
B: I was a lab technician.
A: That's great! We need people with that experience. How long did you do that?
B: From 1991 to 1998.

B. PAIR WORK.   Now use the word bank or your _own_ words.

A: So, _____, what did you do in _____?
B: I was _____.
A: That's great! We need people with that experience. How long did you do that?
B: _____.

A. **Read the ad about positions at Memorial Hospital. Then answer each question yes or no.**

tation includes
nical experience
onths of full-time
d/Surg. Salary:
9 BSN: $19.2
ve compensation
ackage

ICU/DCU
ation: Salem, OH
: Full-time Night
$2500 sign on
time positions on
h $1250 sign on
st have Ohio RN
lary: $18.89 +
upon experience
Comprehensive

Memorial Hospital

Nursing Positions

Full-time and part-time jobs available
RNs – FT and PT up to $36/hour
CNAs – FT and PT up to $16.50/hour

Other Positions

Lab techs – FT   Physical therapists – PT
Dietary aides – FT   Service aides – FT and PT

At least one year experience required for all positions.
Call 704-555-6600.

RN
Lo
Descriptio
position
bonus. P
all shifts w
bonus. Mu
license.
depende
Benefits

RN-N
Full-time po
for RN New
month ori
classroom
as well as
days on M
ADN: $18

1. Can CNAs make $36 an hour? _____

2. Are the lab technician positions part-time? _____

3. Do you need experience for the dietary aide positions? _____

4. Does the hospital have any pharmacist positions available? _____

B. **Answer the questions about jobs at Memorial Hospital. Then practice the conversations with a partner.**

1. A: How much money can I make as a certified nursing assistant?

   B: _____

2. A: Do I have to work full-time if I want to be a service aide?

   B: _____

3. A: How do I apply for a physical therapist position?

   B: _____

C. **ROLE PLAY.   With a partner, create a conversation. Ask and answer questions about jobs at Memorial Hospital.**

END OF WORKPLACE PLUS 1

WORKPLACE PLUS 2

Unit 1

➤ Word bank

Holiday	Date	Seasons
New Year's Day	January 1	Spring (March 20–June 20)
Valentine's Day	February 14	Summer (June 21–September 22)
Mother's Day	Second Sunday in May	Fall / Autumn (September 23–December 21)
Memorial Day	Last Monday in May	Winter (December 22–March 19)
Father's Day	Third Sunday in June	
Independence Day	July 4	**Other words**
Labor Day	First Monday in September	a reality board
Thanksgiving	Fourth Thursday in November	confused
Christmas Day	December 25	remember

DO IT YOURSELF!   **Add your own words to the lists.**

_____   _____   _____

➤ Conversations

❶ Talk about weather and clothes.

A. Read the conversation with a partner.

A: Oh, hi, Susan. What's it like outside?
B: It's cool and rainy.
A: Do I need a sweater?
B: Yes, I think so.

B. PAIR WORK.   Now use your own words.

A: Oh, hi, _____. What's it like outside?
B: It's _____.
A: Do I need _____?
B: Yes, I think so.

❷ Offer to take a message. Leave a message.

A. Read the conversation with a partner.

A: Oakwood Long-Term Care.
B: Hello. Is Carl Green there?
A: No, I'm sorry. He's not in his room right now. Who's calling?
B: This is Pat Green. When will he be back?
A: I'm not sure. Would you like to leave a message, Ms. Green?
B: Yes. My number is 555-9872.

B. PAIR WORK.   Now use the places and people in the box or your own ideas.

Memorial Hospital   Riverview Long-Term Care   Joanne Vargas   Harry Chung

A: _____.
B: Hello. Is _____ there?
A: No, I'm sorry. _____'s not in _____ room right now. Who's calling?
B: This is _____. When will _____ be back?
A: _____. Would you like to leave a message, _____?
B: Yes. My number is _____.

A. Sometimes older patients are confused. Healthcare facilities use reality boards to help confused patients remember everyday information. Look at the reality boards.

Today is

| MONDAY |
| AUGUST | 20 | 2001 |

The season is

SUMMER

The weather is

AND

The next holiday is

Today is

| THURSDAY |
| JANUARY | 31 | 2002 |

The season is

WINTER

The weather is

AND

The next holiday is

Answer the questions.

1. What information is included in a reality board? _____

_____

2. What is a reality board used for? _____

_____

3. Who uses a reality board? _____

B. Create statements for a healthcare worker to say to a patient. Use the information in the reality boards.

1. _____

2. _____

3. _____

C. Create a reality board for today.

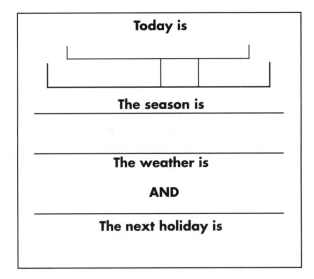

Today is

The season is

The weather is

AND

The next holiday is

Unit 2

➤ Word bank

Kinds of facilities
a long-term care facility
an assisted living facility

On-site services and amenities
a beauty salon   a garden
a barber shop   a library
a whirlpool
an aqua therapy pool

Other words
the grounds   visit
a path   provide
a price   pleasant
a resident   reasonable
a senior

DO IT YOURSELF!   **Add your <u>own</u> words to the lists.**

_____   _____   _____

_____   _____   _____

➤ Conversations

❶ Talk about the facility.

A. Read the conversation with a partner.

A: I have a few questions about this facility.
B: Sure.
A: Is there a garden on the grounds?
B: Yes, right outside the cafeteria.
A: And what about a bus stop?
B: Yes, there's a bus stop down the street.

B. PAIR WORK.   Now use the word bank or your <u>own</u> words.

A: I have a few questions about this facility.
B: _____.
A: Is there a _____ on the grounds?
B: Yes, _____.
A: And what about a _____?
B: Yes, there's a _____.

❷ Ask about on-site services.

A. Read the conversation with a partner.

A: I'm looking for a long-term care facility for my mother.
B: Well, there's one on Main Street.
A: Is it a good one?
B: Yes, it has a beauty shop and an exercise room.
A: Can I see it?
B: Sure. Just call and make an appointment.

B. PAIR WORK.   Now use the word bank and your <u>own</u> words.

A: I'm looking for _____ facility for _____.
B: Well, there's one on _____.
A: Is it a good one?
B: Yes, it has _____.
A: Can I see it?
B: _____. Just call and make an appointment.

A. **Read the ad for the Sunshine Assisted Living facility.**

At Sunshine, we provide residents with a pleasant environment. Our facility includes a garden and pleasant paths for walking. We also have an exercise room with a whirlpool, exercise classes, and movement therapy. On-site services include a beauty salon, a convenience store, and a post office. All services are included at Sunshine at a very reasonable price. Call or visit us today!

Sunshine Assisted Living
7211 Martindale Ave.
Torrence, WV 99312
(304) 555-1452

Write <u>true</u> or <u>false</u> next to each sentence.

1. _____ The Sunshine facility is a school.

2. _____ The Sunshine facility is for children.

3. _____ There is a whirlpool at the Sunshine facility.

4. _____ Residents at Sunshine can walk outside.

5. _____ A reasonable price is a high price.

B. **Ask and answer questions about the information in the ad. Then practice the conversation with a partner.**

1. A: Where is Sunshine Assisted Living?

   B: _____

2. A: What on-site services does Sunshine provide?

   B: _____

3. A: Can you please tell me about the exercise room?

   B: _____

C. ROLE PLAY. **With a partner, create a conversation using the information in the ad.**

Unit 3

➤ Word bank

Equipment	Problems	Equipment	Problems	Actions
a washbasin	is full	a drawer	won't open	fill
a bedpan	is empty	a walker	won't close	empty
a urinal		a chair alarm	doesn't work	
a bedside commode		a bed alarm	is stuck	
a pitcher		a wheelchair		
a cup				
an emesis basin				
an incontinence pad				

DO IT YOURSELF!   Add your own words to the lists.

_____   _____   _____

_____   _____   _____

➤ Conversations

❶ Talk about a problem and solve it.

A. **With a partner, read the conversation between a supervisor and a nurse's aide.**

A: Sharon, can you please check Mrs. Martin?
B: Sure. What's the problem?
A: I'm not sure. I think her bedpan is full. Can you empty it?
B: No problem. I'll empty it now.

B. **PAIR WORK.**   **Now use the word bank or your own words.**

A: _____, can you please check _____?
B: Sure. What's the problem?
A: _____. I think her _____. Can you _____ it?
B: _____. I'll _____ it now.

❷ Talk about a problem and schedule a repair.

A. **With a partner, read the conversation between a nurse and a patient.**

A: Nurses' station. Can I help you?
B: I have a problem. My drawer won't open.
A: What room are you in?
B: 215.
A: OK. Mary is coming now.

B. **PAIR WORK.**   **Now use the word bank or your own words.**

A: Nurses' station. Can I help you?
B: I have a problem. My _____.
A: What room are you in?
B: _____.
A: OK. _____ is coming now.

A. Read the personal care chart notes.

Room	Name	Special notes for nurse's aide
210	Mary Martinez	Provide a bedpan every two hours.
213	Sam Peterson	Check the bed alarm every hour.
214	Linda Garrett	Provide water. Fill the pitcher at 10:00 and 2:00.
217	Nancy Kim	Replace the incontinence pad every hour.
218	Henry Romero	Check the drawers every day for food.

Write <u>yes</u> or <u>no</u> after each sentence.

1. The patient in room 214 needs water at 10:00 and 12:00.   _____

2. Ms. Martinez needs a bedpan every two hours.   _____

3. The nurse's aide has to replace Ms. Kim's washbasin every day.   _____

4. The nurse's aide has to check the bed alarm in room 213 every hour.   _____

5. The aide has to check the drawers in 218 every day for water.   _____

B. Practice giving instructions to a co-worker.

1. Co-worker: What do I have to do in room 214?

   You: _____

2. Co-worker: What do I have to do for Mr. Peterson?

   You: _____

3. Co-worker: What do I have to do in room 217?

   You: _____

C. ROLE PLAY.   With a partner, create a conversation. Ask for and give instructions. Use the personal care chart in Exercise A.

Unit 4

➤ Word bank

Oral care	Nail care	Hair care	Bath care	Other words
toothpaste	an emery board	shampoo	soap	personal hygiene
a toothbrush	nail clippers	conditioner	lotion	a tub
floss	a nail file	a comb	deodorant	a bed bath
mouthwash		a brush		

DO IT YOURSELF!   **Add your <u>own</u> words to the lists.**

_____   _____   _____

_____   _____   _____

➤ Conversations

❶ Talk about personal care and identify products needed.

A. With a partner, read the conversation between co-workers.

A: I'm going to help Mrs. Richards with her hair care. What do I need?
B: You need shampoo and conditioner.
A: Anything else?
B: Yes, a brush or a comb too.

B. PAIR WORK.   Now use the word bank or your <u>own</u> words.

A: I'm going to help _____ with _____. What do I need?
B: You need _____.
A: Anything else?
B: Yes, _____ too.

❷ Talk about personal care products.

A. Read the conversation with a partner.

A: Excuse me. I'm looking for mouthwash. Can you help me?
B: Sure, Mr. Landon. Which one do you want?
A: The one in the green bottle.
B: Here you go.

B. PAIR WORK.   Now use the word bank or your <u>own</u> words.

A: Excuse me. I'm looking for _____. Can you help me?
B: Sure, _____. Which one do you want?
A: The one _____.
B: Here you go.

A. **Look at the patient's personal hygiene record.**

Personal hygiene

Name: Tanya Richards   Room: 104 West

Date: July		1	2	3	4	5	6	7	8	9	10	11	12	13	14	15	16	17	18	19	20	21	22	23	24	25	26	27	28	29	30	31
Bed bath		✓		✓		✓		✓			✓		✓		✓		✓				✓		✓		✓		✓					
Whirlpool tub										✓						✓										✓						
Shower									✓											✓										✓		
Shampoo / beauty salon							✓							✓							✓						✓					
Nail care				✓			✓			✓			✓			✓			✓			✓			✓			✓			✓	
Oral care	AM	✓	✓	✓	✓	✓	✓	✓	✓	✓	✓	✓	✓	✓	✓	✓	✓	✓	✓	✓	✓	✓	✓	✓	✓	✓	✓	✓	✓	✓	✓	✓
	PM	✓	✓	✓	✓	✓	✓	✓	✓	✓	✓	✓	✓	✓	✓	✓	✓	✓	✓	✓	✓	✓	✓	✓	✓	✓	✓	✓	✓	✓	✓	✓

Check each question yes or no.

		yes	no
1.	Did Ms. Richards have a bed bath on July 12?	☐	☐
2.	Did she have nail care on July 18?	☐	☐
3.	Did she have oral care every morning?	☐	☐
4.	Did she have a shampoo every time she had a bath?	☐	☐

B. **Now ask and answer questions about the patient's personal hygiene record.**

1. When did Ms. Richards have a shower?

_____

2. Did she usually have a shower or a bed bath?

_____

3. Which kind of care did she have more often, nail care or oral care?

_____

C. ROLE PLAY.   **With a partner, create a conversation. Ask and answer questions about Tanya Richards's personal hygiene record.**

Unit 5

> ### Word bank

Activities	*Things needed*
a movie	glasses
a class	a pencil
a trip to the mall	a wallet
a trip to the grocery store	a list
a trip to the pharmacy	a prescription
a trip to the library	a library card
a trip to the bowling alley	

DO IT YOURSELF!   **Add your own words to the lists.**

_____   _____   _____

_____   _____   _____

> ### Conversations

❶ Talk about a departure time.

A. **With a partner, read the conversation between a patient and a healthcare worker.**

A: Can I still make the trip to the mall?
B: Yes. There's still time. Do you need to get your wallet?
A: No. I already have it.
B: It's late. You should hurry.

B. **PAIR WORK.**   **Now use the word bank or your own words.**

A: Can I still make _____?
B: Yes. There's still time. Do you need to get your _____?
A: No. I already have _____.
B: It's late. You should hurry.

❷ Talk about departure times and activity schedules.

A. **With a partner, read the conversation between a patient and a healthcare worker.**

A: Did the van to the mall leave yet?
B: Yes, you just missed it. It left five minutes ago.
A: Oh, no. When's the next trip?
B: On Monday.

B. **PAIR WORK.**   **Now use the word bank or your own words.**

A: Did the van to the _____ leave yet?
B: Yes, you just missed it. It left _____.
A: Oh, no. When's the next trip?
B: _____.

A. Look at the trip schedule at Mission Oaks Nursing Home. Then complete each sentence with the correct place.

Mission Oaks Nursing Home

Schedule				September 2 – September 8			
	Sunday	Monday	Tuesday	Wednesday	Thursday	Friday	Saturday
9:00 a.m.	bowling alley		mall		pharmacy		grocery store
1:00 p.m.		library		grocery store		mall	

1. On Sunday there's a trip to the _____.

2. On Monday there's a trip to the _____.

3. On Wednesday there's a trip to the _____.

4. On Thursday there's a trip to the _____.

B. Answer questions about the schedule. Then practice the conversation with a partner.

1. A: What time is the trip to the grocery store on Saturday?

   B: _____

2. A: Which days can patients go to the mall?

   B: _____

3. A: When is the trip to the library?

   B: _____

C. ROLE PLAY.   With a partner, create a conversation. Ask and answer questions about the trip schedule in Exercise A.

Unit 6

➤ Word bank

Linen closet items	Supply room items	Medical equipment
a sheet	a specimen jar	an IV pole
a pillowcase	a wastebasket	an IV pump
a towel	a basin	a blood pressure cuff
a washcloth	a shower cap	a stethoscope
a blanket	dental floss	a bedside commode

DO IT YOURSELF!   **Add your <u>own</u> words to the lists.**

_____   _____   _____

_____   _____   _____

➤ Conversations

❶ Ask for and do a favor.

A. With a partner, read the conversation between two healthcare workers.

A: Could you please get me some sheets from the linen closet?
B: I'd be glad to. Anything else?
A: No. Thanks for the help. I appreciate it.
B: Anytime.

B. PAIR WORK.   Now use the word bank or your <u>own</u> words.

A: Could you please get me _____ from the _____?
B: _____. Anything else?
A: No. Thanks for the help. I appreciate it.
B: Anytime.

❷ Get supplies.

A. With a partner, read the conversation between two healthcare workers.

A: I'm going to the medical equipment department. I need an IV pole.
B: Actually, I do too. Could you get me one when you're there?
A: Sure. I'll be right back.
B: Thanks a million.

B. PAIR WORK.   Now use the word bank or your <u>own</u> words.

A: I'm going to the _____. I need _____.
B: Actually, I do too. Could you get me _____ when you're there?
A: _____. I'll be right back.
B: _____.

A. Look at the stores requisition from Memorial Hospital. Answer the questions.

Memorial Hospital Stores Requisition

Floor: Second West   Date required: 2/3/03

Quantity		Description	price	per	amount
Wanted	Delivered				
48		toilet paper	9.50	24	19.00
30		toothbrushes	6.25	10	18.75
5		boxes of gloves	3.95	1	19.75
20		specimen jars	12.30	20	12.30

Memorial Hospital Stores Requisition

Floor: Third West   Date required: 2/3/03

Quantity		Description	price	per	amount
Wanted	Delivered				
24		toilet paper	9.50	24	9.50
40		dental floss	2.25	10	9.00
40		specimen jars	12.30	20	24.60
5		boxes of gloves	3.95	1	19.75
20		combs	.25	1	5.00

1. Which floor needs 24 rolls of toilet paper?   _____

2. Which floor needs combs?   _____

3. Which floor needs toothbrushes?   _____

B. Now answer questions about the stores requisitions.

1. How many boxes of gloves does Third West need? _____

   _____

2. What supplies does Second West need? _____

   _____

3. Which floor needs more toilet paper, Second West or Third West? _____

   _____

C. Read the paragraph. Then fill out a stores requisition form. Use the prices in Exercise A and today's date.

You work on Third East at Memorial Hospital. You need 24 rolls of toilet paper, 10 boxes of gloves, 60 specimen jars, 10 combs, and 10 toothbrushes.

Memorial Hospital Stores Requisition

Floor: _____   Date required: _____

Quantity		Description	price	per	amount
Wanted	Delivered				

Unit 7

➤ Word bank

Rules in a healthcare facility
Do not smoke in the building.
Do not smoke near oxygen.
Do not forget to wear gloves.
Do not operate the mechanical lift alone.
Do not talk about patients' problems.

Shifts
first / second / third shift
an eight-hour shift / a twelve-hour shift

DO IT YOURSELF! Add your <u>own</u> words to the lists.

_____   _____   _____

_____   _____   _____

➤ Conversations

❶ **Advise someone not to break the rules.**

A. With a partner, read the conversation between two healthcare workers.

A: I have a question. What will happen if I talk about patients' problems?
B: I'm not sure. But it's against the rules. You'd better not.
A: Really? Well, thanks for telling me.
B: Anytime.

B. PAIR WORK. Now use the word bank or your <u>own</u> words.

A: I have a question. What will happen if I _____?
B: _____. But it's against the rules. You'd better not.
A: _____? Well, thanks for telling me.
B: _____.

❷ **Offer a choice.**

A. With a partner, read the conversation between a supervisor and healthcare worker.

A: Would you rather work the first shift or the second shift?
B: That's a good question. I'd better check with my husband.
A: OK. But I need to know soon.
B: Can I tell you tomorrow?
A: Sure. Tomorrow's fine.

B. PAIR WORK. Now use the word bank or your <u>own</u> words.

A: Would you rather work _____ or _____?
B: That's a good question. I'd better check with _____.
A: _____. But I need to know soon.
B: Can I tell you _____?
A: Sure. _____'s fine.

A. **Read the request for a time schedule change at Mission Oaks Nursing Home. Then check each question _true_ or _false_.**

REQUEST FOR TIME SCHEDULE CHANGE

Both individuals requesting change must sign this form and give date of change request.

Today's date: 9/31/03

Name	Floor	Shift	Change date	Present shift hours	to	Requested shift hours
Calvin Booker	3	1	10/9	7 a.m.–3 p.m.	→	3 p.m.–11 p.m.
Grace Chen	3	2	10/9	3 p.m.–11 p.m.	→	7 a.m.–3 p.m.

	true	false
1. Calvin Booker and Grace Chen work on the third floor.	☐	☐
2. The first shift is from 7 a.m. to 3 p.m.	☐	☐
3. The second shift is from 3 a.m. to 11 a.m.	☐	☐
4. Grace Chen is going to work from 7 a.m. to 3 p.m. on October 9.	☐	☐

B. **Now answer questions about the request for a time schedule change.**

1. Who usually works the first shift? _____

2. Who is requesting a change in shift? _____

3. On what date do the people want a change in shift? _____

C. **Read the paragraph. Then fill out the request for a time schedule change.**

Sandra Lopez usually works the third shift, from 11 p.m. to 7 a.m., on the second floor. Two weeks from today, she wants to work the first shift, from 7 a.m. to 3 p.m. Helene Burton works the 7 a.m. to 3 p.m. shift on the second floor, and she has agreed to change with Sandra for that date.

REQUEST FOR TIME SCHEDULE CHANGE

Both individuals requesting change must sign this form and give date of change request.

Today's date: _____

Name	Floor	Shift	Change date	Present shift hours	to	Requested shift hours
					→	
					→	

Unit 8

➤ Word bank

Actions	Vital signs and other indicators	Other words
fall	fluid intake / output rate	beats per minute
trip	respiration rate	breaths per minute
start a fire	blood pressure	
blow a fuse	temperature	
break the equipment	pulse rate	
hurt someone	weight	
gain / lose weight		

DO IT YOURSELF!   **Add your <u>own</u> words to the lists.**

_____   _____   _____

_____   _____   _____

➤ Conversations

❶ Warn someone about a danger.

A. Read the conversation with a partner.

A: Watch out!
B: Why? What's wrong?
A: That's dangerous. You might trip.
B: You're right. Thanks for warning me.
A: You're welcome.

B. PAIR WORK.   Now use the word bank or your <u>own</u> words.

A: _____!
B: Why? What's wrong?
A: That's dangerous. You might _____.
B: You're right. Thanks for warning me.
A: _____.

❷ Remind someone to do something.

A. With a partner, read the conversation between healthcare worker and a supervisor.

A: How often should I check a patient's respiration rate?
B: It's on the patient chart. It's important. Don't forget.
A: I won't.
B: And remember to check the patient's pulse rate too.
A: Don't worry. I will.

B. PAIR WORK.   Now use the word bank or your <u>own</u> words.

A: How often should I check a patient's _____?
B: _____. It's important. Don't forget.
A: I won't.
B: And remember to check the patient's _____ too.
A: _____. I will.

A. Look at the patients' monthly records for June. Then complete the sentences.

Monthly Record (measured June 10)						
(B/P = blood pressure, P = pulse, R = respiration, T = temperature)						
Room	Name	Weight	B/P	P	R	T
227	Smith	142.6	140/64	88	21	96.4
228	Matsuko	157.8	100/50	90	20	97.7
229	Reyes	197.2	136/60	76	22	98.3
230	Lowery	89.4	120/70	112	24	98

1. Anna Lowery weighed _____ pounds.

2. Jenny Smith had a pulse rate of _____ beats per minute.

3. Ron Matsuko had a temperature of _____.

4. Luis Reyes had a respiration rate of _____ breaths per minute.

B. Read the paragraph. Then complete the patients' monthly records for July.

Mr. Matsuko weighed 163.5 pounds and had a blood pressure reading of 120/77.
The patient in room 230 had a pulse rate of 80 and a respiration rate of 21 breaths per minute.
Luis Reyes's temperature was 100.3 and he had a blood pressure reading of 115/70.
The patient in room 227 had a pulse rate of 62.

Monthly Record (measured July 10)						
(B/P = blood pressure, P = pulse, R = respiration, T = temperature)						
Room	Name	Weight	B/P	P	R	T
227	Smith	138.1	135/65		25	98.3
228	Matsuko			90	22	97
229	Reyes	195		78	20	
230	Lowery	92	120/70			98.6

C. Now answer questions about the monthly records for June and July.

1. Who lost weight between June and July?

_____

2. Which patient had the lowest blood pressure in June?

_____

3. In July, did Mr. Matsuko's blood pressure go up or down?

_____

Unit 9

➤ Word bank

Hospital credit union services

a share or savings account   an IRA account
a checking account   a loan
a money market savings account   a mortgage

DO IT YOURSELF!   **Add your own words to the lists.**

_____   _____   _____

_____   _____   _____

➤ Conversations

❶ Use a hospital credit union. Ask for information.

A. With a partner, read the conversation about hospital credit union services.

A: Excuse me. I'd like to open a money market savings account.
B: Certainly. Just fill out this form. Take it to Member Services.
A: Oh. By the way, what is the interest rate?
B: I'm not positive. I'll check.

B. PAIR WORK.   Now use the ideas in the box.

open an IRA account	open a savings account
apply for a loan	apply for a mortgage

A: Excuse me. I'd like to _____.
B: Certainly. Just fill out this form. Take it to Member Services.
A: Oh. By the way, what is the interest rate?
B: I'm not positive. I'll check.

❷ Ask how long something will take.

A. With a partner, read the conversation about hospital credit union services.

A: I'm interested in opening a savings account.
B: OK. Why don't you have a seat? I'll be with you in a minute.
A: By the way, how long will it take?
B: It won't take long. About 15 minutes.

B. PAIR WORK.   Now use the ideas in the box.

opening a checking account	opening a money market savings account
applying for a mortgage	applying for a credit card

A: I'm interested in _____.
B: _____. Why don't you have a seat? I'll be with you _____.
A: By the way, how long will it take?
B: It won't take long. _____.

A. Look at the share withdrawal slip from Memorial Hospital Credit Union. Then check the information that is on the slip.

```
SHARE WITHDRAWAL          INST. # 7356429
                          ACCT. # 23470933

Date    4/15/03        Name    Charlotte Brant

Signature X  Charlotte Brant

                              Dollars      Cents

                                    83      15
          Amount

      Thank You for Using Memorial Hospital Credit Union!
```

1. ☐ the customer's name
2. ☐ the customer's address
3. ☐ the date

4. ☐ the amount of the deposit
5. ☐ the amount of the withdrawal
6. ☐ the customer's account number

B. Now answer the questions.

1. What is the customer's account number?

_____

2. How much money does the customer want to withdraw?

_____

3. What is the date on the withdrawal slip?

_____

C. Read about lab technician Charlotte Brant's expenses. Then fill out her share withdrawal slip. Use today's date.

Ms. Brant needs money for the following expenses:

a new lab coat	$10.00
comfortable shoes	$20.00
a prescription refill	$12.79
physical therapy	$75.00

```
SHARE WITHDRAWAL          INST. # _____
                          ACCT. # _____

Date  _____    Name  _____

Signature X  _____

                              Dollars      Cents



          Amount

      Thank You for Using Memorial Hospital Credit Union!
```

Unit 10

➤ Word bank

Health problems	Training for healthcare workers	Other words
Alzheimer's disease	in-service training on health problems	a premium
diabetes	cardiopulmonary resuscitation (CPR)	life insurance
arthritis	infection control	a beneficiary
heart disease	orientation to the facility	
stroke	how to order medical equipment	
emphysema		

DO IT YOURSELF!   **Add your <u>own</u> words to the lists.**

_____   _____   _____

_____   _____   _____

➤ Conversations

❶ Break news. Express surprise and approval.

A. **With a partner, read the conversation between healthcare workers.**

A: Hey, Betty, guess what!
B: What?
A: We're going to have an in-service training on diabetes.
B: No kidding. That's terrific. When is it?
A: Next Monday.

B. **PAIR WORK.**   **Now use the word bank or your <u>own</u> words.**

A: Hey, _____, guess what!
B: What?
A: We're going to have an in-service training on _____.
B: No kidding. That's terrific. When is it?
A: _____.

❷ Remind someone about an obligation.

A. **With a partner, read the conversation between healthcare workers.**

A: Have you signed up for the in-service training on arthritis yet?
B: No, I haven't. Not yet.
A: Well, we're supposed to do that by 3:00 today.
B: I know. Thanks for reminding me.

B. **PAIR WORK.**   **Now use the word bank or your <u>own</u> words.**

A: Have you signed up for the in-service training on _____ yet?
B: No, I haven't. Not yet.
A: Well, we're supposed to do that by _____.
B: I know. Thanks for reminding me.

A. Mission Oaks Nursing Home is offering its employees a new life insurance plan. Read the application for a life insurance plan.

MEMORIAL LIFE INSURANCE APPLICATION FORM

1. My telephone number _____
                (Area code)   Number

Name _____

Address _____

City, State, Zip _____

Sex ☐ M ☐ F   Age _____   Date of birth _____
                                                              Mo.   Day   Year

2. I wish to apply for life insurance coverage under   ☐ $5,000.00 plan   ☐ $2,000.00 plan

3. I have enclosed $_____ to pay for my first month's premium for the plan checked above.

4. My beneficiary (person to be paid at death) is: _____
                                                   First name   Middle   Last name   Relationship to injured

5. My signature X _____ Date _____ / _____ / _____
                                                                   Mo.   Day   Year

Read about the monthly payments.

$2,000.00 PLAN Monthly Premium

Age	30	31–35	36–40	41–45	46–50	51–55
Male	$7.64	$8.66	$10.68	$12.76	$15.32	$21.04
Female	$6.50	$7.38	$8.96	$10.08	$11.96	$16.66

$5,000.00 PLAN Monthly Premium

Age	30	31–35	36–40	41–45	46–50	51–55
Male	$17.60	$20.15	$25.20	$30.40	$36.80	$51.10
Female	$14.75	$16.95	$20.90	$23.70	$28.40	$40.15

Check each question <u>true</u> or <u>false</u>.

	true	false
1. A monthly premium is the amount you have to pay every month.	☐	☐
2. The beneficiary is the person who pays for the insurance.	☐	☐
3. A 37-year-old male who has the $5000 plan has to pay $25.20 per month.	☐	☐
4. A 42-year-old female who has the $2000 plan has to pay $12.76 per month.	☐	☐

B. Fill out the form for yourself. Compare forms with a partner.

END OF WORKPLACE PLUS 2

Common abbreviations

ac	before meals	**ER**	emergency room	**min**	minute
ADL	activities of daily living	**F**	Fahrenheit	**ml**	milliliter
a.m.	morning	**fl**	fluid	**mm**	millimeter
amb	ambulatory	**ft.**	foot	**NA**	nursing assistant
amt	amount	**gm**	gram	**oz.**	ounce
bid	twice a day	**h (hr)**	hour	**P**	pulse
BM	bowel movement	**ht**	height	**p.m.**	after noon
BP	blood pressure	**in.**	inch	**R**	respiration
C	centigrade, Celsius	**kg**	kilogram	**RN**	registered nurse
cc	cubic centimeter	**l**	liter	**T**	temperature
cm	centimeter	**lb.**	pound	**tbsp**	tablespoon
CNA	certified nursing assistant	**liq**	liquid	**w/c**	wheelchair
		LPN	licensed practical nurse	**wt**	weight
		m	meter	**yd.**	yard

Metric conversions

Linear Measurements

Metric	English (approx)	English	Metric (approx.)
1 mm	.04 in.	1 in.	2.5 cm
1 cm	.4 in.	1 ft. = 12 in.	30 cm
1 m	1.09 yd./39 in.		

English	Metric (approx.)	English	Metric (approx.)
3′ =	90 cm	5′6″ =	165 cm
4′ =	120 cm (1.2 m)	5′7″ =	167.5 cm
5′ =	150 cm (1.5 m)	5′8″ =	170 cm (1.7 m)
5′1″ =	152.5 cm	5′9″ =	172.5 cm
5′2″ =	155 cm	5′10″ =	175 cm
5′3″ =	157.5 cm	5′11″ =	177.5 cm
5′4″ =	160 cm (1.6 m)	6′ =	180 cm (1.8 m)
5′5″ =	162.5 cm		

Volume

English	Metric
1 fluid ounce	29.6 milliliter (ml)
1 pint	.47 liter (l)
1 quart	.95 liter
1 gallon	3.8 liter

Weight

Metric	English	English	Metric
1 gm	.04 oz.	1 oz.	28.4 gm
1 kg	2.2 lb.	1 lb.	0.45 kg

English	Metric
100 lbs.	45 kg
125 lbs.	56.25 kg
150 lbs.	67.5 kg
175 lbs.	78.25 kg
200 lbs.	90 kg

Temperature

Celsius	Fahrenheit
5/9 (F – 32°)	9/5 (C + 32°)
0° = freezing	32° = freezing
37° = normal body	98.6° = normal body
100° = boiling	212° = boiling

Answers are provided for the Authentic practice exercises that have specific answers. For those exercises that require an individual response, evaluate each answer for responsiveness, completeness, and correctness of expression.

WORKPLACE PLUS 1

Unit 1
Authentic practice
Exercise A
1. no   2. yes   3. no   4. no

Exercise B
1. (She's) A nurse.
2. (She's a) Nursing assistant.
3. He's an escort.

Unit 2
Authentic practice
Exercise A
1. C   2. A   3. B   4. B   5. C

Exercise B
1. It's on C hall / next to the elevator / across from the recreation room.
2. It's on A hall / next to the chapel / across from the shower room.
3. It's on C hall / next to the radiology department / next to the emergency room / between the radiology department and the emergency room / across from the waiting room.

Unit 3
Authentic practice
Exercise A
1. yes   2. yes   3. no   4. no

Exercise B
1. Press 6 plus 3327.
2. Press 9 plus (the) area code plus (the) telephone number.
3. Turn the handle to the left.

Unit 4
Authentic practice
Exercise A
1. purple   2. gray   3. pink   4. It's wrinkled.

Exercise C

Name: Mr. Franklin			Room: 457
Item	Color	Please wash	Please press
undershirt	white	☒	☐
shirt	purple	☒	☒
pajamas	gray	☒	☐

Unit 5
Authentic practice
Exercise A
1. c   2. a   3. e   4. b   5. d

Exercise B
1. Monday at 2:30 p.m.   3. Drawing.
2. In the recreation room.

Unit 6
Authentic practice
Exercise A
1. true   2. false   3. false   4. true

Exercise B
1. No (there isn't).   3. Carrots and peas.
2. Yes (there are).

Unit 7
Authentic practice
Exercise A
1. Ricky Martin   3. Brenda Leonard
2. Hailemichael Kidane   4. Marsha Gooden

Exercise B
1. (You have to) Clean the lounge and supervise the dining room meal.
2. Clean the shower room and pass ice on A hall.
3. (I have to) Assist with feeding in the dining room.

Unit 8
Authentic practice
Exercise A
1. no   3. yes
2. no   4. yes

Exercise B

```
┌─────────────────────────────────────────────────────────────┐
│   TO REPORT A SERIOUS ACCIDENT IMMEDIATELY OR FOR QUESTIONS,   │
│        PLEASE CALL RISK MANAGEMENT AT 555-3222                 │
├─────────────────────────────────────────────────────────────┤
```
1. Name of person injured: _James Braxton_   2. Sex: ☑ male   ☐ female

ACCIDENT
3. Date: _5/15/03_   4. Time: _2:30 p.m._   5. Location: _Bathroom/room 411_

6. FALLS
☐ while walking   ☐ while standing   ☐ from chair / wheelchair
☐ from bed / stretcher   ☑ in bathroom

7. INJURY (check all that apply)
☑ fracture   ☐ sprain   ☐ cut   ☑ bruise

No. 487
DATE _____

PAY TO THE ORDER OF _Vista Card_ $ | 16.55 |
Sixteen and 55/100 _____ DOLLARS

United Bank
1550 Fourth Ave.
Sacramento, CA 95819

MEMO _Vista Card (bill)_ _____

1:041000689:1 60660668' 487

Unit 9
Authentic practice
Exercise A
1. Dr. Denise Kitterman.   3. Shoes.
2. August 20, 2003, or 8/20/03.   4. $24.99.

Unit 10
Authentic practice
Exercise A
1. no   2. no   3. yes   4. no

Exercise B
1. (You can make) Up to $16.50 per hour.
2. No, you don't.
3. Call 704-555-6600.

WORKPLACE PLUS 2

Unit 1
Authentic practice
Exercise A
1. The day of the week, the date and year, the season, the weather, the next holiday.
2. (A reality board is used) To help confused patients remember everyday information.
3. Healthcare workers and patients (use a reality board).

Exercise B
Answers will vary but may include the following:
   What's the day / date / weather today?
   What season is it?
   What is the next holiday?

Unit 2
Authentic practice
Exercise A
1. false   2. false   3. true   4. true   5. false

Exercise B
1. (It's at) 7211 Martindale Avenue, Torrence, West Virginia 99312.
2. A beauty shop, a convenience store, and a post office.
3. The exercise room has a whirlpool, exercise classes, and movement therapy.

Unit 3
Authentic practice
Exercise A
1. no   2. yes   3. no   4. yes   5. no

Exercise B
1. (You have to) Provide water and fill the pitcher at 10 and 2.
2. (You have to) Check the bed alarm every hour.
3. (You have to) Replace the incontinence pad every hour.

Unit 4
Authentic practice
Exercise A
1. no   2. yes   3. yes   4. no

Exercise B
1. (She had a shower on) July 9, 19, 29.
2. (She usually had) A bed bath.
3. Oral care.

Unit 5
Authentic practice
Exercise A
1. bowling alley   3. grocery store
2. library   4. pharmacy

Exercise B

1. (The trip to the grocery store on Saturday is at) 9 a.m.
2. (Patients can go to the mall on) Tuesday and Friday.
3. (The trip to the library is on) Monday.

Unit 6
Authentic practice

Exercise A

1. Third West
2. Third West
3. Second West

Exercise B

1. (Third West needs) 5 (boxes of gloves).
2. (Second West needs) (48 rolls of) Toilet paper, (30) toothbrushes, (5 boxes of) gloves, and (20) specimen jars.
3. Second West (needs more toilet paper).

Exercise C

Memorial Hospital Stores Requisition

Floor: Third East   Date required: _____

Quantity		Description	price	per	amount
Wanted	Delivered				
24		toilet paper	9.50	24	9.50
10		boxes of gloves	3.95	1	39.50
60		specimen jars	12.30	20	36.90
10		combs	.25	1	2.50
10		toothbrushes	6.25	10	6.25

Unit 7
Authentic practice

Exercise A

1. true   2. true   3. false   4. true

Exercise B

1. Calvin Booker (usually works the first shift).
2. Calvin Booker and Grace Chen (are requesting a change in shift).
3. (The people want a change in shift on) October 9.

Exercise C

Monthly Record (measured July 10)
(B/P = blood pressure, P = pulse, R = respiration, T = temperature)

Room	Name	Weight	B/P	P	R	T
227	Smith	138.1	135/65	62	25	98.3
228	Matsuko	163.5	120/77	90	22	97
229	Reyes	195	115/70	78	20	100.3
230	Lowery	92	120/70	80	21	98.6

Unit 8
Authentic practice

Exercise A

1. 89.4   2. 88   3. 97.7   4. 22

Exercise B

Name	Floor	Shift	Change date	Present shift hours	to	Requested shift hours
Sandra Lopez	2	3		11 p.m.–7 a.m.	→	7 a.m.–3 p.m.
Helene Burton	2	1		7 a.m.–3 p.m.	→	11 p.m.–7 a.m.

Exercise C

1. (Jenny / Ms.) Smith and (Luis / Mr.) Reyes (lost weight between June and July).
2. (Ron / Mr.) Matsuko (had the lowest blood pressure in June).
3. (In July, Mr. Matsuko's blood pressure went) Up.

Unit 9
Authentic practice

Exercise A

Students should check items 1, 3, 5, 6.

Exercise B

1. (The customer's account number is) 23470933.
2. (The customer wants to withdraw) $83.15.
3. (The date on the withdrawal slip is) 4/15/03 or April 15, 2003.

Exercise C

SHARE WITHDRAWAL

INST. # 7356429
ACCT. # 23470933

Date _____   Name Charlotte Brant

Signature X *Charlotte Brant*

	Dollars	Cents
Amount	117	79

Thank You for Using Memorial Hospital Credit Union!

Unit 10
Authentic practice

Exercise A

1. true   2. false   3. true   4. false